My
Grieving Journey
Book

Donna and Eve Shavatt

Paulist Press
New York/Mahwah, N.J.

We dedicate this book to our mother . . .
who somehow managed to raise seven kids alone
while suffering through the loss of her husband and parents.

And to our father . . .
who died when we were very young,
and whose loss inspired us to write this book to help others.

And to all of you who have felt the pain of losing a loved one.
May this book help you throughout your grieving journey.

Special thanks to Sheena Shannon and all of the
incredible people at The Caring Place in Pittsburgh, PA.

Cover and interior design and graphics by Saija Autrand, Faces Type & Design

Copyright © 2001 by Donna Shavatt and Eve Shavatt

Library of Congress Cataloging-in-Publication Data:

Shavatt, Donna, 1959–
    My grieving journey book / by Donna Shavatt and Eve Shavatt.
        p. cm.
    Summary: Provides information, advice, and activities to help young people deal with the death of someone they love.
    ISBN 0-8091-6695-X
    1. Grief—Juvenile literature.   2. Loss (Psychology)—Juvenile literature.
    3. Bereavement in children—Juvenile literature.   [1. Death.   2. Grief.]
    I. Shavatt, Eve, 1955–   II. Title.

BF575.G7 S47 2001
155.9'37—dc21

2001036334

Published by Paulist Press
997 Macarthur Boulevard
Mahwah, New Jersey 07430

www.paulistpress.com

Printed and bound in the
United States by Versa Press, East Peoria IL
September 2014

Table of Contents

How to Use Your Grieving Journey Book

My sister and I lost our father when we were very young, so we know that this is a hard time for you right now.

Losing a loved one can bring out *lots* of feelings, some that you've never had before. These feelings are normal, but they can be scary and confusing. This book was written to help you learn how to deal with them. You may not have every feeling we describe, or you may have many more feelings than we could fit. Either way is normal.

To use this book, you can start at the beginning and read through to the end, then go back and choose the part you want to work on.

Or you can start by picking the balloon on the cover that seems to match the way you're feeling. Then find the matching balloon in the table of contents. It will tell you what page to look on. When you open to that page, you'll find help in understanding the way you feel.

When you are finished reading, go to the next page to write or draw about your feelings.

You can return to different balloons again and again, depending on how you feel each day.

May you always have caring friends and family during your grieving journey.

Donna and Eve

I miss
you

    A really hard part about someone dying is that you miss them so much. You might miss the way they talked to you or the way they held you. You might miss their face, or their smell, or their voice.

    Tell a caring grown-up about these things that you miss. Someone may be able to hold you the same way, or talk to you the same way, and that may make you feel better.

    Try writing down the things you miss about your loved one. Keep a picture of them close to you or something that reminds you of them like a key chain, a scarf, or a piece of jewelry. And remember, thinking of them will not always hurt so badly.

Use this page to list all the things you miss most
about the person you lost.

I feel
sad

Feeling sad is something everyone feels at times. When someone you love dies, it can make you feel saddest of all.

Tell the people in your life how you are feeling. If you feel so sad that you just can't stand it, tell a grown-up right away. Never do anything hurtful to yourself, no matter how sad you feel. There are things that other people can do to help you.

Just talking about being sad may help you feel better. Or you may want to go to a safe room and cry for awhile to get the sadness out. Or you may want to write about it, or draw a picture that shows how sad you feel.

It is important to remember that you won't always feel so sad. Being sad is a part of grief and also a part of healing.

When you feel sad, use this page to write or draw about it.

I don't believe it

When someone dies, sometimes people just don't want to believe that it really happened.

When you feel like this, you may tell yourself and others that your loved one is not really gone. You may feel that he or she will be back home soon. It is just so hard to believe that this person could be gone forever.

Your family and friends will try to help you understand that your loved one really did die. This may make you angry, because you don't want to hear that right now.

There will come a time when you will be ready to accept what has happened.

If you can, write some of the reasons why you don't believe what has happened.

I don't feel
anything

Another normal thing that may happen after the death of a
loved one is to not feel anything at all about it. This is called
"shock" and just means that you were hurt so badly by the death
that your mind and your body wanted to stop feeling that bad.
It's a little bit like when your dentist numbs your mouth to fix
a cavity. For a while, you can't really feel your lips.

This numb feeling, or shock, will go away, and your feelings
will come back when your mind and body feel that you can handle
them. It's just another way you are trying to get used to this loss.

Write or draw about how you don't feel anything now. You could draw your body and the parts that feel numb, like from the dentist.

I can't stop crying

Crying is one way to get hurt feelings out. We have tears inside us for just this reason. Letting out your tears can even help keep your body from getting sick.

Some people think that crying makes you seem like a baby. Many boys especially think this. But it is really a very strong and brave thing to do. It is also a very healthy way to deal with things that upset you.

If you feel as if you can't stop crying, that's okay. If you can, go to a quiet place and take lots of tissues! Cry as much as you need to. Having a caring grown-up hold you while you cry is very helpful, too.

Think of the tears that are coming out as a way of washing some of your sadness away!

Write or draw about how you are feeling now.

I can't cry
at all

Some people, after a loved one dies, can't seem to cry at all.

If you aren't able to cry, you might worry that people will think you didn't really care about the person you lost.

This is not true. The body has many ways to deal with painful feelings. Some people feel that they are drowning in an ocean of tears. Other people feel all dried up inside like a desert. Everyone feels grief a little bit differently.

You don't need to try to force yourself to cry. When your tears are ready to come, they will.

Write or draw about how it feels if you are not able to cry now.
You could try to draw your face with tears and without tears.

It's my
fault

Some people worry that they were the cause of their loved one's death. Perhaps when they got angry at the loved one, they said or thought, "I hate you!" or "I wish you were dead!"

If you said or thought something like this, it does not mean that you caused the person to die. A lot of us say things like that when we get angry.

Your loved one knew that you were just angry, that you didn't really mean what you said, and that you didn't really want the person to die.

If you have been thinking that what happened is your fault, you may be afraid to tell those taking care of you about it. But it is very important that you tell them, so that you can work through these feelings together.

The person's dying had nothing to do with anything you thought or said or did.

Thinking it or wishing it cannot make it happen!

If you feel that the person's dying was your fault, use this page to write or draw the reasons why you feel this way.

I don't feel good

Because our bodies are connected to our minds, when we think a certain way it makes our bodies feel a certain way.

When you're upset about losing your loved one, your body may feel upset too. You may hurt in your head, or your heart, or your stomach—or all over your whole body.

Always tell a grown-up when you don't feel well. And remember that you can help your body by talking about your feelings. Keeping your feelings all trapped inside can make your body start to feel sick. Talking, drawing, running, punching your bed or pillow, and writing down your thoughts are all great ways to help your body feel better.

When you feel sick or in pain, use this page to write about it.
Or try drawing your body and the places that hurt.

I'm
scared

You may be feeling scared since your loved one died. There is nothing wrong at all with feeling scared, especially at a time like this. Everyone feels scared sometimes!

You may worry that the person or people who take care of you now will die too. But there are many people who care about you and love you, and you will always be taken care of. Most people live a long, long time and live to be really, really old.

Tell those who care about you that you are scared. Explain to them how you feel. You may find that just telling someone will make the scared feelings go away. The people who are taking care of you plan to take care of you until you are all grown up and can take care of yourself.

Write or draw about all the things you are scared of now.
Show them to a grown-up when you are ready.

I have
bad dreams

Bad dreams, or nightmares, are something most of us have, especially when a loved one dies. When we have bad dreams, we wake up feeling very scared and upset.

Bad dreams are a way your mind uses to let feelings out while you sleep. Bad dreams are not real. They are like watching a scary movie on TV and can never hurt you.

Keeping a night-light on in your room, or sleeping with a teddy bear or other stuffed animal can help you when you wake up. Talking to someone afterwards can also make you feel better or even make the dreams stop. If you can't find words to describe your dreams, try to draw a picture of them. And at night, right before you go to sleep, try to think of things that make you feel relaxed and peaceful. This sometimes can help you have better dreams.

Remember when you wake up that it was *only* a dream. It was not real.

You can write about your dreams here, or draw a picture of them.

I'm mad!

Many times people feel mad or angry when someone they love dies.

If you feel mad, you may think it's wrong to feel that way because the person couldn't help dying. But it is okay to feel angry that they left you. That anger will go away. You can help to get it out of your body in many ways.

You must never hurt yourself or anyone else to help anger go away. Here are a few good ways to get rid of it: Go into a safe room and scream for as long as you want, or punch your fists against your bed or a pillow, or find a place where you are allowed to run and run as fast and hard as you can. Talking about your anger can also make it go away. These are safe ways to help get that anger right out of your body.

When you feel mad, use this page to write or draw what you feel!

I wasn't
always sad

When your loved one was still alive, there were probably
lots of things you liked to do. You might have enjoyed writing,
reading, drawing, or playing with a favorite toy. You might have
used a computer, played video games, helped cook dinner, or
watched TV.

Outside activities might have been fun too. Playing with
friends from school or your neighborhood, roller blading, playing
sports, climbing trees, building forts, or swimming could have
been just some of the outdoor things that you liked to do.

All the things that you used to do will one day be fun again.
Little by little, you will return to the activities that once brought
you joy.

Use this page to draw or write about some of the activities you used to like, when you weren't feeling so sad.

I'm feeling better

As you write, draw, talk, and find other ways of helping yourself, there will be times in between the sadness and anger and tears when you begin to feel better. After feeling better for a while, you may go back to feeling sad or upset once more, then back again to feeling better.

As time passes, the good feelings will happen more and more often. If you have been crying a lot, you may find that on some days you don't feel like crying at all. You may want to play with your friends or toys again. It is good and healthy to let yourself have fun when this happens. Having fun does not mean that you are forgetting the person who died, or that you don't still love him or her.

The time will come when you will smile more and more, and you'll be happy once again.

Write or draw the ways you feel better, or the new things you feel more like doing now.

I believe in
something
more

When a loved one dies, some people believe that the person is now with God in heaven. They believe that God loves each of them during life and that he continues to love each of them after death. Some people were taught this growing up as part of their religion. Other people come to believe this on their own.

Still others do not believe in God or that the loved one is in heaven. Instead, they believe that their loved one lives on inside their heart.

If you grew up in a particular religion, you might want to visit a church, synagogue, or mosque and talk to someone there. Ask a caring grown-up to take you. If you did not grow up in a particular religion, there may be another place very special to you that makes you feel there is something more than what you can see or hear or touch. Ask someone who cares for you to take you to this place. Until you are able to get there, think of it often.

Use this page to write about what you believe in, or draw a picture of the place that best shows your belief.

I am forever
connected

Even when we lose someone very special to us, we still have other relatives who make up our family.

Can you think of all *your* relatives? Some of them may be as close as the next room, and you see them every day. Others may be in different states, even different countries! Some relatives lived in the past. Though they never met you, just the thought of you probably made them very happy. And finally, you have relatives waiting in the future.

No matter where or when your relatives live, or lived, they are part of your family, and you are always connected to them!

On the Family Tree below, put your name on one of the blank leaves in the middle. Then fill in the other blank leaves with the names of your family members. You may need to ask an older family member for help. Think of as many relatives as you can. Go back as far as possible.

35

I am not alone

It is important to remember that there are many people in your life who are special to you, and who think of you as special to them, even if you are not related.

Who are they? Your school teacher, piano teacher, karate teacher, your friends and their families, your neighbors, babysitters, daycare workers, your counselor, your doctor, your dentist, the librarian, the bus driver, the mail carrier, and dozens of other people you meet during your life. You may not know everyone on this list right now, but you probably know many of them.

Having people you know in your world can make you feel less alone. These people can be like an extended family. An extended family is a family made up of all those you feel are special to you.

Look around and think of all the people you know or would like to know. Put your name in the center, then fill in the petals around you with all the special people in your world!

I need to say goodbye

When you are feeling better, you may find it helpful to say goodbye to your loved one.

One way to do this is to write them a letter or draw them a picture. Say things like "I love you" or "I miss you," or express any other feelings that you have about the person. At the end, you can tell them goodbye.

You can put the letter in your memory box, mail the letter to someone special to hold for you, or keep the letter anywhere that you choose.

Saying goodbye is a way to move on. You still love that person just as much, and you will never forget them. But you have many things you want to do as you grow up. Know that your loved one, although gone from this earth, will remain close to you in your heart and in your thoughts, for always.

Use this page to write your goodbye letter or to draw a goodbye picture.

The ABC's of Healing

Always remember that you are loved.

Bad dreams help get rid of bad feelings and cannot hurt you.

Cry as much or as little as you need to.

Death is part of the cycle of life.

Eat healthy, exercise, and take good care of yourself.

Friends can be very helpful during this sad time.

Good things will happen to you again.

Have a special toy or doll or stuffed animal to hold or hug.

If you don't feel well, always tell a grown-up.

Jumping, running, and playing can make you feel better.

Keep reminders of your loved one in a special place.

Love yourself; there is no one in the world exactly like you.

Mad feelings go away faster if you help them get out.

Never hurt yourself or anyone else.

One day you will be able to say goodbye, and you will feel better again.

Put your thoughts down on paper as often as you can.

Quiet time is a way to think about what is happening to you.

Remember that feelings keep changing all the time.

Sadness is very normal and will soften in time.

Try to draw how you feel—don't worry about how it looks.

Understand that you did not cause your loved one's death.

Visit family and friends and other people who care for you.

Wishing someone dead cannot make it happen.

XOXOXO is a good way to send your hugs and kisses on paper.

You will get through this time of grief.

Zest for life, which means feeling happy, will come back to you!

40

I'm afraid
I'll forget

As time passes, you may become afraid that you'll forget your loved one.

But even though you may not think of the person every day, it does not mean that you have forgotten them. They are in your heart forever.

Loved ones leave reminders of themselves in many ways. You may look like this person, or sound the way they did. You may laugh at the things they found funny, even play or act the way they did. You may like to listen to the same music that they listened to or read the same kinds of books.

There are other reminders that your loved one might leave. You can use an old shirt of theirs to sleep in. You can wear a piece of jewelry that was special to them. You can find a photo of them. All of these things keep them close in your heart.

I can remember with a memory box

A memory box is a great way to collect the things that remind you of the person you lost. You can make it out of an old shoebox, a cookie tin, or a coffee can. A grown-up can even help you make one out of wood. Once you have a box, put your loved one's name on it, maybe using glitter, magic markers, or crayons. Decorate the box any way you like. On the lid, you can put a photo of your loved one or their name in fancy cut-out letters.

Fill your memory box with photos, jewelry, gifts your loved one gave you, their scarf or gloves, words you write about them, or pictures you draw. Now you have a treasured collection that you can keep with you forever. Looking through your memory box can help you feel close to your loved one once again.

On the rest of this page, make a list of the things you want to put in your memory box.

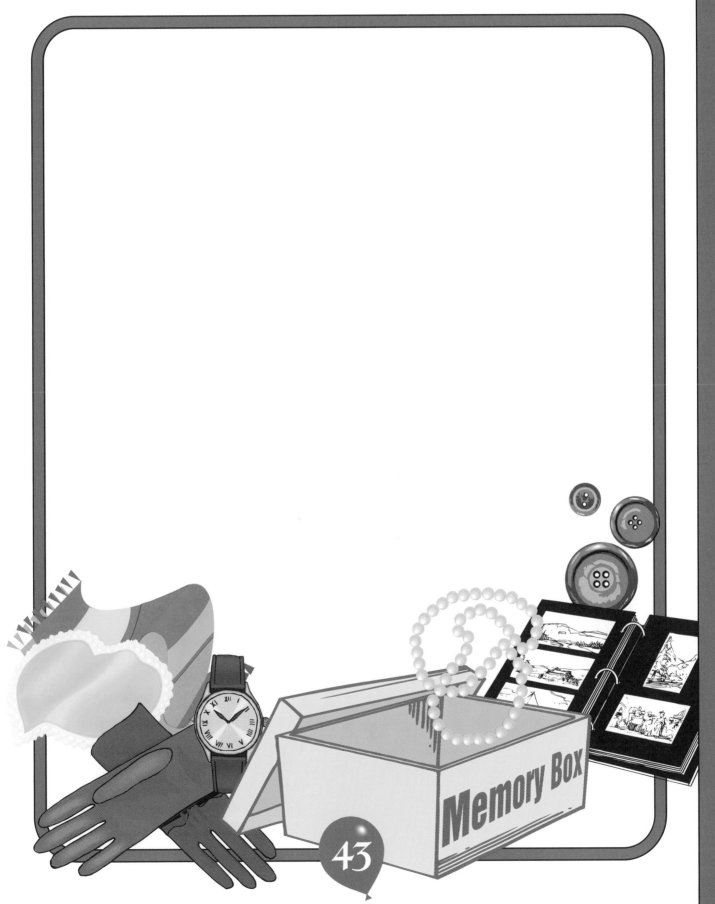

The Healing Heart

Here's a special way to show that you are keeping your loved one forever in your heart. Put your name in the box on the left side of the split heart, and your loved one's name in the box on the right side. Then cut out the two sides and paste the two pieces tightly together on top of the solid heart at the bottom. Keep this treasure in your memory box, under your pillow, in your pocket, or in any special place that you choose. (If you don't want to cut this page, trace the split heart and solid heart on another piece of

Put your name here in this box

Put your loved one's name

Paste the 2 sides tightly together onto this heart

Express Yourself!

Color in these balloons using your special colors.

Photo Album

If you have pictures of your loved one, paste some inside the frames on these two pages. Or you can draw pictures of your own within the frames. You can also create a "word picture" by writing a description that will at once remind you of a special time. For example, "The picnic where it rained so hard the frosting was washed off the cake."

What You Can Do to Help Your Children through This Difficult Time

It is crucial that you take care of your own needs. You need strength to help your child cope with his or her loss, and you won't have this strength without a support system of your own. Children react to *what they see you do*. Locate a support group, a counselor, a member of the clergy, or anyone who can be there just for you. For additional help, look for appropriate books in your library or book stores.

Keep things as routine as possible. Try not to make any more changes in your lives than absolutely necessary at this time.

Talk to your kids. Remember that their imaginations can be worse than reality, so tell them as much as you feel they can handle, as clearly and honestly as you can. Reassure them that they did not cause the loved one's death. Naturally you will want to acknowledge and validate their emotions, but one important exception to this is when a child blames himself or herself for the loved one's death. Turn to the "It's my fault" worksheet in this book for help (page 19). Have the child write down the reasons why he or she feels to blame. Then counter these reasons one by one with clear logic as to why this is simply not so.

Reassure your children that you intend to take care of them until they are all grown up and can take care of themselves. Also reassure them that you are able to take good care of yourself and that you will keep yourself healthy.

Learn methods to help your children express their feelings, such as by having free and open conversations with you and with others. Encourage them to write down their feelings or to draw them. Show them safe and non-hurtful ways to release their anger, such as punching their bed or pillows. Exercise is a wonderful outlet for everyone. Try taking walks together, or playing together at home or at the playground.

Above all, remember that you cannot give away what you yourself do not possess. A great example of this is the instructions given prior to airplane travel: In the event of air loss, always apply your own oxygen mask first, then attend to your children. You cannot help them breathe if you yourself are oxygen deprived. Seek your comfort and strength so that you have it to give to your children.

The methods suggested in this book are presented merely as guidelines. Each of us reacts differently to the grieving process. This book may not cover all emotions or situations. It is intended to be as helpful and informative a tool as possible, but you may need to seek professional care or other outlets as well.

Donna Shavatt
Eve Shavatt